SAY

SAY

SPEAKING GOD'S
PROMISES

ALLYSON MCELROY,
of On3Ministries

XULON PRESS

Xulon Press
2301 Lucien Way #415
Maitland, FL 32751
407.339.4217
www.xulonpress.com

Printed in the United States of America.

Paperback ISBN-13: 978-1-6628-0451-9
Hardcover ISBN-13: 978-1-6628-0452-6
eBook ISBN-13: 978-1-6628-0453-3

Dedication

This book is dedicated to my husband, Michael, whose support of me and faith in me knows no end. I'm forever grateful for his love of God and for his continual focus on our family & our God-given purpose. I love you.

ENDORSEMENTS

I'm so excited to recommend "Say" and would even categorize it as a "must read." It has been said that "the WORD works IF we work the WORD." How true! In this book Allyson helps us understand the power of READING the WORD, APPLYING the WORD, SPEAKING the WORD and LIVING the WORD!! In these difficult times we all need to be reminded to stay focused on God's Word. Thank you for this awesome reminder, Allyson!

~Lynn Wheeler,
Author & Minister and founder
of Lynn Wheeler Ministries

She is your all-American girl-next-door with the drive of a racecar. Through her book "Say" Allyson has a creative way of making a story come to life and drawing the reader in so deeply with her words as if we are her family sitting in her living room. We are no longer reading – we are sitting beside her.

~Debbie Stroman,
360 Degree Coach

SAY

A talented young lady and gifted speaker, Allyson McElroy strikes directly at the heart of personal devotion to Jesus Christ as she inspires the reader to experience real life and to "say" the promises of God, revealed in the Bible.

~Reverend Mick Snider,
International Evangelist
and founder of Mick Snider Ministries, Inc.

Everything that comes to us in life, comes through some type of relationship. Think about it: your job, friends, and family; they are all relationships. When you catch that revelation, you realize the importance of relationships to open the conduit of opportunity and blessing. Fail to build healthy relationships and you close that conduit, leading to failure. What this means is a person can control the quality of their life simply by controlling the quality of their relationships.

Allyson McElroy's new book helps us open the most important relationship conduit of all: our relationship with God. Through her writing we are ushered into the secret place where God can speak to us and connect us with His love. Day by day, as you go deeper into your relationship with God, you will see that growth opening new conduits of revelation of who God is and what He has already done for you. He loves you. I believe through this book you will discover how much you love Him as well.

Endorsements

~Randy Stroman, Leadership and
Relationship Coach
Founder, The Stromans Leadership
and Relationship Coaches

Introduction

Smooshing Life

The first devotional I ever read was by Ruth Bell Graham. I was 16 and was amazed at how motivated and moved I could be by just a few words each day. Don't let that fool you, though. At age 16 I was also driving down dirt roads with no headlights, doing the Macarena and Time Warp, and shoe polishing my friends' cars (see Day 5).

Perhaps smooshing these two versions of me – a love for God's word and a love for family, friends, and life – is just what was needed to create this devotional book, Say.

I pray it equally convicts you and equips you. Makes you laugh and makes you lean in. I pray we will know each other by the end of this book and that in the words of my mentor, Debbie Stroman, you'll "feel like family, just sitting in the family room telling stories."

So pull up a chair – rocking, side, swivel, lawn, or bean bag. Let's take this book day by day then share its truths and laughs with others on our journey.

~Allyson

**Bless the Lord, O my soul, and forget not
all His benefits**—Psalm 103:2 NKJV

BURGER KING SLIDES

OUR TOWN'S ONE-AND-ONLY BURGER KING
had the best playground. Outside, under a shaded cover, a
large red tube enticed youngsters to climb up then over a
massive ball pit to the tube's slide on the other side. And,
if there's anything children of the 80s know, it's this: you
never went to Burger King for the meal (or even the paper
crown). You went for the slide.

Darting out of my mom's brown Pontiac, my friends
and I raced to the play area. Not making it first and not
being one who liked to wait in lines, I came up with an idea.
"Amber," I said to the girl in front of me, "I'll be your best
friend if you let me slide down first."

Wow. What a benefit. All you have to do, Amber, is let
me go first in line and POOF, just like that, you've got a
friend in me. (I'm shaking my head at my younger self, too.)

Of course, as we grow older (er, let's say wiser), we seek
bigger and better benefits. Take travel, for example. If you're
headed to a hotel, you may search out those with a pool,
free breakfast, free WIFI, and nearby parks and entertain-
ment. But what if you check in and just sit on your bed? You

bypass the pool. You forget the breakfast is free and pay for mushy oatmeal at the WaffleHut on the corner. You dare not log in to the WIFI in case you're charged. And, since you can't see the nearby parks from your window, you forget they're there.

Friend, can I tell you that we do this all the time with our faith? We accept salvation and then sit there. We bypass promises of protection. We forget His promises of joy and trade it for hit and miss moments of happiness replaced with worry. We don't "log in" to a relationship with Him for fear we'll "do it wrong" or "not please Him." And, since we can't see promises of peace and love and health, we forget they're there.

Do you know all the promises of God? Do you know the purpose He has for you? Or are you sitting on the edge of your bed, while the blessing and favor of God go unnoticed?

This series of devotions will walk you through what it means to be a Christian and live the awesome life - full of benefits - that God has for you. Are you ready? Turn the page and I'll be your best friend. (just kidding)

If you confess with your mouth the Lord Jesus and believe in your heart that God has raised Him from the dead, you will be saved.—Romans 10:9 NKJV

TORNADOES!

YEARS AGO A STATE-WIDE NEWS PROGRAM had a television show called "Those Terrible Twisters." The Oklahoma-famous Gary England would go from town to town projecting viewer-submitted VHS recordings of close encounters with tornadoes.

My father's claim to fame is a run in with such a storm. I was with him. Standing on our front porch, Daddy hoisted the heavy camera on his shoulder and recorded a tornado that tore up part of our town. He sent in the tape, which ended up on the touring twister show.

Oklahomans are... different. I'm just going to put that out there right now. We like gawking at these storms. There are entire Facebook groups, social media pages, and television shows devoted to the power, the potential devastation, and the awesomeness of thunder and lightning. Why are we okay with watching storms? Because we, for the most part, know the comfort of our shelter. We know where to run for safety.

We can take videos of the wind and play in the rain because we know the power of our protection.

Do you know the power of your Protector? When life's storms come up – and they look different for everyone – do you know who you are and *Whose* you are?

> Your storm doesn't define you. And if you're letting it, let it go.

> Your burdens don't define you. And if you're letting them, let them go.

> Your past doesn't define you. And if you're letting it, let it go.

What defines you, my Christian friend, is your Creator.

So let me ask. Do you know Whose you are? Do you know the authority you have and the power of your Protector? It all starts by believing and following Romans 10:9. This one verse tells how to experience salvation and receive access to all the promises, protection, and authority God has given. This verse says, "If you openly declare that Jesus is Lord and believe in your heart that God raised Him from the dead, you will be saved."

So today, let's make sure you're defined by your Creator and *Savior*. Let's pray aloud: "Heavenly Father, I openly declare that Jesus is Lord and I believe that You raised Him from the dead. Thank You for saving me! Amen."

DAY 3

Whatever is good and perfect is a gift coming down to us from God our Father.—James 1:17 NLT

It's a box!

IF YOU'VE EVER GOTTEN A 4-YEAR OLD NEW tennis shoes, you know what happens. As soon as those sneakers are laced up and feet back on the ground, they start running. And every single 4-year old believes the same thing - those shoes make them run faster.

My husband, Michael, couldn't wait to give our cotton-topped son, Cole, a brand-new pair of the latest and greatest sneakers one Christmas. And, as a 4-year old only child (and only grandchild), the entire room couldn't wait for him to open them.

Ceremonially walking the box over to Cole, Michael stood, waiting for the unwrapping to begin. Cole tore just enough red and green paper back to realize what it was... "It's a BOX!!!" he joyfully exclaimed, as though the box itself was the best gift in the world.

Are you living that way? Are you living as though salvation and the Romans 10:9 experience is all that God gave you? I wonder if God shakes His head like we did at Cole that day.

Because, friend, God has given you so much more than a box, er, uh, salvation! With it, He has an entire box full of promises, blessings, and purpose.

But you have to unwrap it.

His word - the Bible - is filled with details of a life of joy, peace, and healing that He has given you. Did you notice I said *has given* you - past tense? Just like Michael gave the gift to Cole, God has given you the gift of His word. But it means nothing until you open it.

James 1:17 tells us that God gives good and perfect gifts. But, guess what? You have to open them! Let's pray, "Heavenly Father, I pray that we will open Your word and search out all the good promises, blessings, and purpose You have for us. Guide us to them and let us quickly and easily find exactly what You've given us for each day. In Jesus' name, Amen."

Death and life are in the power of the tongue.—Proverbs 18:21 NKJV

"Ruuuuubeeeeennnn!"

"Ruuuuubeennn!!"

I've never been so excited and mad at the same time. In its heyday, American Idol was THE show to watch. Everyone talked about it the next morning and shared our love or hate of the judges' (and America's) decisions.

So when Michael and I had an event the night of the season finale between Ruben Studdard and Clay Aiken, we used our new DVR recording feature and rushed home to push play, long after the actual results had been shared with 38 million Americans.

We were comfy on our couch, ready for endless "we'll find out... after the break" moments when the phone rang. Instead of a hello, I heard a cheer of "Ruben!!!! Can you believe he won!?"

Can someone say spoiler alert? My well-meaning friend's words took me from anticipation and thrill to anger and frustration in a split second.

Words. They have that power. Let me show you:

"It's twins!"

"It's cancer."

"You're hired."

"You're fired."

"Will you marry me?"

The Bible says words have power. Scratch that... it says the *tongue* has power. This means reading words, thinking words, and humming the words to a song don't have near the impact of *speaking* the words. Throughout this book you'll be challenged to say, to speak, to vocalize promises, prayers, and purpose so that whatever you're going through, whatever feelings and emotions arise in you can be immediately changed by words.

Today, I challenge you to pray out loud. For some of you, that's easy. For others, this may be the first time. Let me help. Pray, "Heavenly Father, I praise You today. I pray that the words I speak will be uplifting, encouraging, and bring You glory. In Jesus' name, Amen."

Those who live according to the flesh set their minds on things of the flesh, but those who live according to the Spirit, the things of the Spirit.—Romans 8:5 NKJV

SHOE POLISHING CARS

I CALLED IT A BLONDE MOMENT. 'STILL DO.

I was 16 and ready to semi-destroy a few friends' cars with white, shoe-polished messages and drawings all over their windows. But first, a trip to Walmart for supplies. Being the leader of the group, I marched us toward the back of the store with clear purpose. But no matter how many times I scoured the aisles, I couldn't find shoe polish. "Wait," Rebecca halted, "why are we in the automotive section? Shouldn't we be in the *shoe* aisle?!"

Well, duh. But we were using it for car windows, right?

What made perfect sense to me, well, didn't make sense at all. I needed to think more like the designer of the store (and a normal human being) and less like a 16-year old graffiti artist.

When we experience salvation, our thought life can toggle between thinking like our old selves and thinking like the Christian we have become. The book of Romans calls it "setting our minds" on spiritual things and not fleshly things (things that make sense in the crazy, upside down world).

When we focus our attention on what God says through His word (the Bible), we realize that many promises and benefits and gifts apply to us. We realize that He has equipped us and positioned us to walk through this world, our lives, and every single day and what that day brings with it.

But we must set our minds. We must realize that our thinking may need to be tweaked a bit. We must start thinking like our new selves and not who we once were. We must move our thoughts from one "aisle" to another.

Today, ask God to show you when your mind and thoughts should be moved from an old way of thinking to a new, spiritual way. Let's pray (out loud, remember?): "Heavenly Father, I pray that You will show me when my mind is not on spiritual ways. Show me when I'm limiting my thoughts and mindset to earthly things instead of focusing on what Your word says about my situation. In Jesus' name, Amen."

Since you have heard about Jesus and have learned the truth... throw off your old sinful nature and your former way of life... instead, let the Spirit renew your thoughts and attitudes.—Ephesians 4:21-23 NLT

SCISSORS

SCHOOL SUPPLY TIME. AS A BOY MOM, I LOVE it much more than he does. He's good with using last year's supplies and searching his backpack for pencil stubs. But not mom! No, I still remember carefully writing his name on each package of crayons (the 64 pack, of course), packs of glue sticks, and the Super Mario lunchbox.

I found a box of his preschool supplies up in a storage shelf recently and it took me back! There, buried beneath the colored pencils and markers, was a pair of blue, round tipped, capped scissors, just sharp enough to cut a heart out of construction paper. Wow... did his little fingers ever fit in those holes? Was he a little bit scared the first time those (dull) blades cut through bright red paper?

When we first start our Christian walk (or re-start or get on the right track), we may need to cut some things out of our lives. Some things we've been doing that don't line up with God's promises.

In fact, if, since you've been reading this, you've felt a little confusion or "yeah, but what about" moments, I encourage you to search what needs to be cut out of your life.

> Something altering your frame of mind, like social media overload?

> Something altering your perception, like a drug or alcohol?

> Something altering your emotions, like a negative friend?

> Something altering your spirit, like an old belief that doesn't line up with your Christ-following decision?

The Word addresses this in Ephesians: "Since you have heard about Jesus and have learned the truth that comes from Him, throw off [cut off] your old sinful nature and your former way of life."

So what is it? What part of your life needs spiritual scissors? Let's pray, "Heavenly Father, I pray that You will show me what is preventing me from fully agreeing with Your promises and walking in Your truth. I ask that You will guide me as I get rid of old ways of thinking and replace them with Your word. In Jesus' name, Amen."

DAY 7

**The Lord is close to all who call on Him,
yes, to all who call on Him in truth.**—
Psalm 145:18 NLT

NOT SO FAST...

I MAY BE SUPER ORGANIZED AND A CLEAN-
freak now, but not as a pre-teen. Nope, it was common for
my clothes to be tossed across the floor, wrappers tucked
in drawers, and my Garfield "My Room, My Mess, My
Business" poster to be dangling by one pushpin. So when
Mom and Dad gave promises of a sleepover with friends, it
came with a two-letter word attached: IF.

> If you clean your room, then you can have
> a sleepover.

> If you don't speed, then you won't
> get a ticket.

> If you complete college, then you will
> get a degree.

Life is full of if/thens. And so is God's word. The big-
gest one, of course, is our Romans 10:9 experience (IF you

openly declare that Jesus is Lord and believe in your heart that God raised Him from the dead, [THEN] you will be saved). At that point, we've done our part (the IF) to receive salvation (the THEN). We have full access to the promises of God!

That's great, but not so fast... I have access to the door to the local bank. But if I don't have the key, then I can't get in. I have access to the food in the fridge. But if I don't open the door, then I won't get any food. You have access to God's promises, but if you don't do your part, then those promises remain waiting. Look for your part (the IF) in these promises:

- James 4:7 Resist the devil, and he will flee from you.
- Hebrews 4:16 Let us come boldly to the throne of our gracious God. There we will receive mercy, and we will find grace to help us when we need it most.
- Matthew 6:33 Seek the Kingdom of God above all else, and live righteously, and He will give you everything you need.
- Proverbs 3:6 Seek His will in all you do, and He will show you which path to take.
- Psalm 91:9-10 If you make the Lord your refuge, if you make the Most High your shelter, no evil will conquer you; no plague will come near your home.

What's stopping you from doing what you need to do to receive the promises? Let's pray, "Heavenly Father, I thank

You for Your promises. I pray that You will give me boldness and wisdom to put my faith in these promises into action so that I may receive the blessing. In Jesus' name, Amen."

DAY 8

The Lord will withhold no good thing from those who do what is right.— Psalm 84:11 NLT

MISCONCEPTIONS

WHEN HE WAS FOUR, I EXPLAINED SALVATION to Cole (you know, the Romans 10:9 concept from earlier?). Well, it just happened to be right after Easter, meaning Jesus dying on a cross and raising back to life for our sins was fresh on his mind.

"Mom," his squeaky little voice said, "I don't want to be saved. I never want to die on a cross!"

I spent the next few moments assuring him that Romans 10:9 was all it took and that at no point would he have to go near - let alone die - on a cross. I thought he understood.

Fast forward a year to us driving home from church. He's in the backseat, buckled in and peering out the window. I can see in my rear view mirror that his eyes are a bit misty when I hear "Mom, I'm ready to die on a cross and be saved."

This time, he believed me when I told him that Jesus died on the cross so he didn't have to, and I led him in a prayer to become a Christian.

Wow. I'm still speechless as I retell this story. So much weight to what my little boy thought!

But what about you? What weighs heavily on your mind as I mention "promises from God"? What misconceptions do you have about your Heavenly Father?

Does the term "Heavenly Father" put memories of an abusive, earthly father in your mind?

Do you see God, seated on a towering throne marking red checks by your name with each mistake you make? Do you believe every sniffle and stubbed toe is a punishment for the little lie you let slip last week?

I hope I can reassure you like I did Cole when I say that God is *for* you. God is on your side. God wants these promises for you, and it's so important that you believe that before we move on to the next few pages. Let me pray for you and with you: "Heavenly Father, I pray that my friend (I) will realize how much You love them (me) and want good for them (me). I believe You love them (me) and are on their (my) side. In Jesus' name, Amen."

DAY 9

He lifted me out of the pit of despair, out of the mud and mire. He set my feet on solid ground and steadied me as I walked along. —Psalm 40:2 NLT

WEATHER DOODLES

DID YOU EVER RECEIVE AN ASSIGNMENT IN school that was so stress-filled, so challenging, that it brought bats - not butterflies - in your stomach? Yes, that was me in first grade. Prepared with a black crayon and sheet of white paper, it was time to draw the weather picture that might - just may - be featured in an upcoming issue of The Ada Evening News. (Oh, to have the "stresses" of first grade again!)

No matter the forecast, the local newspaper would feature a stick-figure type drawing of the upcoming sunny, rainy, or snowy day. The poor parents (literally and figuratively poor) would spend a quarter each morning to see if their child's drawing was selected. (Spoiler alert - everyone's got selected at some point.)

If you were to pick up a crayon and draw the emotional, spiritual, mental, and physical weather of your life, what would it look like? A round sun popping from behind a cloud? A scribbly windstorm? Or maybe a page dotted with rain and puddles?

SAY

As much as I'd like to draw each day with a rainbow, let's face it - we go through stuff! We walk through the rain and even get stuck in the "mud and mire," as the Psalms say.

But He lifts us out! He steadies us! How? How does He - in Heaven - do this? Through His word. The promises of God do not fail. They are our umbrella in a rainstorm, our jacket in the cold, and a shelter in tornado season.

But just like you'd better buy a raincoat before the sprinkles start, it's important that we know the promises - and how to receive them - *before* our muck and mire experience.

Today, ask God to reveal to you a promise that you need for today. Then, pick up His word and seek it out. Let's pray: "Heavenly Father, as I read Your Word, I pray that You will show me exactly what I need for this moment. In Jesus' name, Amen."

DAY 10

Your love for me is very great.—
Psalm 86:13 NLT

LOVE LETTERS

I'M NOT SURE WHY A 14-YEAR OLD GIRL WAS teaching Sunday school, but she was. That girl was me, and my class was comprised of 4th grade, wanna-be-cool pre-teens. One Sunday morning after the opening prayer, I whispered a secret to them all: I found a love letter in the room.

The girls all squealed and even the boys looked a bit curious as I read a few lines. "Your love for me is great" and "I have loved you with an everlasting love" (Jeremiah 31:3).

I'll be honest. All pre-teen girls want a boy to like them, so they were a bit disappointed and eyes began to roll when they found they'd been duped by me. The love letter wasn't from the hottie of the day... it was from Someone much greater.

There are times in life when we want to be loved. We want to feel loved. We want acceptance and companionship. With God, though, we are never alone. His word (aka His love letter) says over and over that He loves us.

You may not feel it today - or ever. But if you ever need a promise that you are never alone, write these verses down. This is just a small part of God's love letter to you:

Romans 8:31-39 and Hebrews 13:5 (*with a bit of explanation added by me*)

...God is for us. Who can ever be against us? Who will condemn us? No one - for Christ Jesus died for us and was raised to life for us... Can anything ever separate us from Christ's love? Does it mean that He no longer loves us if we have trouble or calamity, or are persecuted, or hungry, or destitute, or in danger, or threatened with death? No, despite all these things, overwhelming victory is ours through Christ Jesus, who loved us... Nothing can ever separate us from God's love. Neither death nor life, neither angels nor demons, neither our fears for today nor our worries about tomorrow - not even the power of hell can separate us from God's love. No power in the sky above or in the earth below - indeed nothing in all creation will ever be able to separate us from the love of God that is revealed in Christ Jesus our Lord. For God has said, "I will never fail you. I will never abandon you."

Let's pray, "Heavenly Father, thank You for loving me. When I don't feel loved or when I feel alone, I will remember Your promises and know You are faithful. In Jesus' name, Amen."

DAY 11

Be joyful. Grow to maturity. Encourage each other. Live in harmony and peace. Then the God of love and peace will be with you.—2 Corinthians 13:11 NLT

BUMPER STICKERS

MY NANNY AND PAPA HAD AN OLD, TWO-TONE Chevy truck that they'd drive to a town in Missouri called Branson. Being "country folk," they loved the music shows that Branson had to offer. (For those of you who know Branson, think a 1980s version - not a now version). What I remember most about that truck and their trip are the bumper stickers they'd plaster all over the tailgate. Every music show they visited end up with its rectangular sticker on the tailgate of that pickup truck.

I've seen your bumper stickers, too. You 26.2 Marathoners, you Moms of Honor Roll Students, and you Jeep waving Dads. I've seen your family stickers, dog loving stickers, and brand supporting stickers. And each window or bumper or tailgate tells exactly who you are in one short, sweet phrase or graphic.

If, just suppose, that the words from your mouth and the actions you showed each day were bumper stickers, what would we know about your life? Do you need to get out a scraper and remove a few (start acting and talking a different way)? Do you need to add a few for those friends who don't know who you represent (God)?

God's word in 2 Corinthians 13:11 addresses our bumper stickers (hang with me here). He gives a few commands. Simple. Short. They could fit on a bumper sticker, and each tells about how we should show God's love:

- Be joyful.
- Grow to maturity.
- Encourage each other.
- Live in harmony and peace.

If these spiritual bumper stickers aren't on your tailgate (uh, you know what I mean), then let's pray that they will be.

"Heavenly Father, I pray that I will exemplify You. I pray that when others hear and see me that they will see someone joyful, growing in You, encouraging, and someone living in harmony and peace. In Jesus' name, Amen."

Your word is a lamp to my feet and a light to my path.—Psalm 119:105 NKJV

SWINGING LANTERNS

I ALWAYS WANTED ONE OF THOSE OLD TIMEY lanterns. You know, the ones with a hook at the top and glass surrounding a match-lit wick? I pictured myself swinging it back and forth in front of each step and exploring some great forest. Or my tiny backyard at night, I guess.

The thing about a lantern is it only shows you what's in front of you. You can't see 50 feet ahead. You may not be able to tell if the bridge is out a mile down the path. And you won't know about that apple orchard with ripe produce ready for you to pick until you're right up on it.

Psalms tells us that God's word is a lamp (no electricity back then, so we'll go with the image of a lantern on this). God's word is not a massive torch to light up the road ahead. It's there to guide you one step at a time. One verse at a time. One prayer at a time. One devotion at a time. Spiritually, you may not be ready for the road hazard or the awesome fruit buffet that is ahead!

As we reflect back on this week's devotions, consider each day that God, through His word, has revealed to you another step in your Christian walk.

Maybe He's revealed to you that serving Him (Romans 10:9) gives full access to promises and benefits (Psalm 103:2). Maybe you've discovered the power in your words (Proverbs 18:21) and now know the importance of lining up those words and thoughts with a spiritual life (Romans 8:5). Or maybe you've felt a tug to really know His promises (James 1:17) and to erase misconceptions about His love (Psalm 84:11).

As we get deeper into this book, allow God to shine His light on each step. Allow His word to draw you closer to Him. And fully believe each promise as you pray (out loud), "Heavenly Father, I believe that You are guiding me. I believe I am drawing closer to You and learning more about You. Show me exactly what I need to see. In Jesus' name, Amen."

**The Lord makes firm the steps of the one
who delights in Him.**—Psalm 37:23 NIV

THE BRIDGE

AFTER SUNDAY SERVICES AS A CHILD, MY
entire family would drive to a local cafeteria for lunch. The
Village Inn Cafe always promised 3 things: A cigarette
vending machine where I could pull tiny knobs and hear
the springs boing-boing back to me, gravy-soaked smoth-
ered steak, and multiple trips around "the bridge."

The bridge was nothing more than a brick planter sit-
uated around two columns that held up the building's
awning. And, after I was full from lunch, Daddy would
take me out and walk me around and around the 3-foot-
tall bridge, holding my hand the entire way.

I smile as I reflect on this memory. Feeling so tall, yet so
sure that I wouldn't fall.

I get this same feeling when I read a promise in Psalm
37:23. "The Lord makes firm the steps of the one who
delights in Him. Though he may stumble, he will not fall,
for the Lord upholds him with His hand."

What are you saying about your journey? What
words are you proclaiming over tomorrow's walk and the

steps you'll take next week? What are you speaking over your future?

Because God - in His infinite wisdom - gave you a promise to speak. This promise means He will guide you. This promise means you will not fall. This promise means He will direct your steps.

Let's speak it together. "Heavenly Father, I thank You that You guide and direct my steps. I thank You that You will not let me fall. I delight in my walk with You and love You. In Jesus' name, Amen."

For we are God's masterpiece. He has created us anew in Christ Jesus, so we can do the good things He planned for us long ago.—Ephesians 2:10 NLT

A Scribbled Mess of a Masterpiece

Have you ever seen a little girl run, excitedly, to her mommy with a waxy mess of a crayon drawing? "Mommy, mommy! Look what I drew! Do you know what it is?"

Let's face it. We have no idea what it is. A horse on a rocket? An elephant with seven trunks? A deflating beach ball? But Sophie knows exactly what it is. And she's so proud. She can't wait to show it off to mommy and you and everyone who walks by. Because *she created it*.

God created you. No matter what others think of you, no matter how they try to define you, you can only be defined by your Creator, and He's pleased with His creation.

His promises apply to YOU. And here's what He thinks of you:

- 2 Corinthians 5:17 – Anyone who belongs to Christ has become A NEW PERSON. THE OLD LIFE IS GONE; A NEW LIFE HAS BEGUN!
- Ephesians 2:10 – For we are GOD'S MASTERPIECE. He has CREATED us ANEW IN CHRIST JESUS, SO we [I] CAN DO THE GOOD THINGS HE PLANNED FOR us [ME] LONG AGO.
- John 15:15 – Now you are [JESUS'] FRIENDs, since I have told you everything the Father told me.
- Psalm 139:14 – I praise You for I am FEARFULLY AND WONDERFULLY MADE.
- Romans 6:6 – We know that our old self was crucified with Him in order that the body of sin might be brought to nothing, so that we would NO LONGER be ENSLAVED TO SIN.
- Romans 8:2 – For the law of the Spirit of life has SET you FREE IN CHRIST JESUS FROM THE LAW OF SIN AND DEATH.
- 1 Thessalonians 1:4 – ...God has CHOSEN you to be His own people.

Now here's your "say" assignment. Go back through each verse and add "I am" before each phrase in all caps. Read them out loud. I am a new person. I am God's masterpiece. Say it. Keep saying it until you've gotten it. Share it with your teenagers, your children, your small group. We've got to know Whose we are before we can know who we are!

Let's pray: "Heavenly Father, thank You for creating me on purpose, for a purpose. Thank You for giving me new life. Thank You for planning good things for me. Thank You for setting me free from sin. I love You. In Jesus' name, Amen."

DAY 15

Fix your thoughts on what is true, and honorable, and right, and pure, and lovely, and admirable. ...Take captive every thought to make it obedient to Christ.—Philippians 4:8 NLT and 2 Corinthians 10:5 NIV

NOSE PICKERS

COLE IS MY 13-YEAR-OLD, SUPER LOGICAL, hilarious, best-in-the-world son (#provemewrong). You know how most little kids pick their noses? Cole NEVER did. I mean never. If he saw another kid in kindergarten doing it, he'd start gagging. So, if we went to a friend's house for dinner, I never added "don't pick your nose" to a list of etiquette reminders. Sure, "don't pass gas" was in there, but never "don't pick your nose." Why? Because he wasn't prone to do it. It wasn't a part of who he was and is.

Just like I know the ins and outs of my son, God, too, knows the ins and outs of His children. Over and over throughout His word He gives us a list of reminders. The one at the top? Don't worry/fear not/don't be afraid. (See Philippians 4:6, Proverbs 12:25, Isaiah 41:10, and many more) He knew we'd be super prone to let our thoughts wander toward the what ifs.

This is especially true when life gets stormy. Just like we can see the lightning and hear the thunder of an April shower, so, too, can we see and hear an emotional, mental, spiritual, and physical storm in life. It's easy to let our thoughts focus on the storm.

All this week, recognize those times when your mind wanders. His word says in Philippians 4:8, "Fix your thoughts on what is true, and honorable, and right, and pure, and lovely, and admirable. Think about things that are excellent and worthy of praise."

When your thoughts begin to shift to worry and fear and the what-ifs, follow 2 Corinthians 10:5 that says to "capture rebellious thoughts and teach them to obey Christ."

"Fix" and "Capture" are two action words. Let these actions start with prayer: "Heavenly Father, please make me aware of when my thoughts aren't fixed on good things. Father, let me quickly capture those thoughts and line them up with Your words and Your promises. I realize this is my responsibility and I commit to capturing worry-filled and fearful thoughts today. In Jesus' name, Amen."

Do not conform to the pattern of this world, but be transformed by the renewing of your mind. Then you will be able to test and approve what God's will is. —Romans 12:2 NIV

POOR VICKY

THE RUNNING JOKE IN OUR HOUSEHOLD - OR should I say in our car - is that the GPS voice means nothing when Michael is driving. Vicky the Voice, as we call her, can say "in half a mile, turn right onto Main Street." Before you know it, she's saying, "recalculating" or "please make a legal U turn." See, Michael gets super caught up in a story he's telling or in a news report on the radio or even in his own thoughts and tunes Vicky out. Poor Vicky.

Just like staying focused on Vicky and the road and the news report all at the same time requires intention, so, too, does staying focused on God's word, truths, promises, and purpose.

Ephesians 6:12 says something that rattles our human brains a bit: "We are not fighting against flesh-and-blood enemies, but against evil rulers and authorities of the unseen world, against mighty power in this dark world, and against evil spirits in the heavenly places."

Let me explain. As much as we want to think we're fighting against Monday's doctor's report, Tuesday's bad boss, Wednesday's fight with our teenager, Thursday's speeding ticket, and Friday's toothache... we're not. We're fighting against the distractions they cause and, quite possibly, the destruction they cause (see Proverbs 14:12).

See, the enemy wants you distracted physically so he can attack you spiritually. He wants you distracted by the doctor's report so that instead of turning onto Psalm 91 Street, you'll head straight toward Fear. He wants you thinking so much about getting turned down for the promotion that you miss the turn onto Proverbs 3:6 and, instead, fall into despair without a promise in sight.

Just like the book of Philippians commanded us to "fix our thoughts" and 2 Corinthians told us to "capture our thoughts," the book of Romans gives another command: Transform our minds. Intentionally focus on God's promises. We have no reason to fear a spiritual battle because "the Spirit who lives in us is greater than the spirit who lives in the world" (1 John 4:4).

Let's pray, "Heavenly Father, I thank You that You overcame the world. Your word says Your Spirit within us is greater than the 'mighty powers in this dark world.' Lord, let us focus on You. Let us fix, capture, and transform our minds to line up with Your word. In Jesus' name, Amen."

He leads me—Psalm 23:3 NKJV

VALLEY WALKERS

I FIND THIS ODD COMFORT IN KNOWING THAT good, God-loving people in the Bible had problems. It makes me feel normal. David, for example, said, "Hey, I'm walking through a dark valley," and let us know that he had enemies around him, needed protection, and longed for comfort. But, as though he'd already read the then-unwritten New Testament, David followed our lesson from yesterday.

In Psalm 23 David starts out by saying, "The Lord is my shepherd; I have all that I need." Boom. Period. End of sentence. But then, as if those worrisome thoughts started creeping up, he kept reminding himself that even though life is tough, even though his enemies are around him, look what the Lord has done and is doing!

The Bible never promised a storm-free life. We live in a trouble-filled world. But Jesus addresses this in John 16:33, "Here on earth you will have many trials and sorrows. But take heart, because I have overcome the world." And, again, we're reminded in 1 John 4 that, "You belong to God... the Spirit who lives in you is greater than the spirit who lives in this (trouble-filled, sometimes crazy) world."

Say

So what, then, do we do when we face hardships, battles, and burdens on this Christian walk? Watch for the all-caps command words in these verses:

- Matthew 11:28 – COME TO ME (JESUS), all of you who are weary and carry heavy burdens, and *I will give you rest.*
- James 4:7 – RESIST THE DEVIL, and *he will flee from you.*
- Psalm 91:9-10 If you MAKE THE LORD YOUR REFUGE, if you MAKE THE MOST HIGH YOUR SHELTER, *no evil will conquer you; no plague will come near your home.*

Do you notice that the answer to a prayer is AFTER each command? While promises are ours, they often require us to act, to accept, to do something. So what will you do today to receive a promise?

Let's pray: "Heavenly Father, I thank You for Your promises. Father, I recognize that to receive many promises, I must act. Father, I commit to those actions today. Whatever my need may be, I, too, promise to do my part to receive the benefits of Your promises. In Jesus' name, Amen."

Don't worry about anything; instead, pray about everything. Tell God what you need, and thank Him for all He has done. Then you will experience God's peace.—Philippians 4:6-7 NLT

RECIPES

I HAVE NEVER ONCE GOOGLED A RECIPE AND didn't begin the search with "easy."

"Easy brownies."
"Easy chocolate cake."
"Easy sugar cookies."

Looking at that list, I guess I only Google desserts, ha! But I'm all about the fewest ingredients possible. So finding a cake mix that says "Just add water" is right up my alley!

Recipe for Cake
Step 1: Preheat oven to 350 degrees
Step 2: Pour enclosed mix and 1 cup water into bowl and mix
Step 3: Pour into greased pan and bake 35 minutes
Step 4: Allow to cool
POOF! Just like that, I'll have a cake!

See, we often have to do something before we can receive something, just like I have to do stuff to the cake mix before I get a cake. God is the same way. To receive various promises and gifts from Him, we often must do something. Let's call it following a recipe.

Recipe for Peace (Philippians 4:6-7)
Step 1: Don't worry about anything
Step 2: Pray about everything
Step 3: Tell God what you need
Step 4: Thank Him for all He has done
POOF: Then you will experience God's peace, which exceeds anything we can understand!

Are you following God's recipes?

Let's pray (uh, just a reminder, out loud): "Heavenly Father, today I will not worry about anything. Instead, I will pray about everything and tell You what I need. I thank You for all You've done! Thank You for the peace I'm about to experience! In Jesus' name, Amen."

Be strong in the Lord and in His mighty power.—Ephesians 6:10 NLT

FLEXING MUSCLES

"SHOW ME YOUR MUSCLES!"

Is it instinct that every little boy immediately rolls up his sleeve, grits his teeth, and flexes his non-existent muscle at this command? I think so. Super proud, he may even grunt, "I am strong" or "Hulk Smash!"

Young Hulk (aka - the little boy) may not have any muscle, but he sure thinks he does! He's confident in his "power" and "strength."

There are days you may look like you feel and feel like you look. No offense! But just like you can't see Hulk, Jr's muscles, you can't see your own mental, emotional, spiritual, or physical strength. As we walk this spiritual journey, we're commanded to be "strong in the *Lord* and in *His* mighty power."

You can hide behind His power. You're not expected to fight any single day alone. You're not expected to walk in your own power and strength (or lack thereof). You're to be strong in Him and in His power.

I picture God saying, "Take advantage of me! Don't count on your own strength. I am with you and will never leave you. It's a promise!"

So let me ask. What have you been doing on your own? What battle have you tried to fight, what storm have you tried to walk through, without God?

Flex your spiritual muscles.

Let's pray, "Heavenly Father, You are my strength and power. I have strength to fight the battle and power to walk through the storm because YOU are my strength and YOU are my power. YOU do not fail. Thank You! In Jesus' name, Amen."

Draw near to God and He will draw near to you.—James 4:8 NKJV

FINDING GIRAFFES (THE DEVO ABOUT SEEKING)

IN THE EARLY 90s OUR LOCAL NEWSPAPER announced a city-wide scavenger hunt. Each Tuesday at noon a new clue would be published as to the location of a plastic toy circus animal hidden in the community. Whoever found it, in this case, a giraffe, would win an overnight trip to a state park.

Seriously, y'all. We were on the hunt! We'd camp out at the news office at 11:55 each Tuesday, just waiting for the day's hot-off-the-press paper to make its way to our hands. We couldn't find the prize if we didn't have the clues!

Can I tell you that God, too, is waiting to be found by you? He gives specific clues - we'll call them instructions - on how to find Him. And, here's the kicker, it's not hard to find Him because, spoiler alert, He's not hiding! We've allowed daily life, cares, and concerns to cover Him. We must put aside daily distractions that we've allowed to cloud our view of Him and...

- You will seek Me and find Me, when you search for Me with all your heart. (Jeremiah 29:13 NKJV)
- I love those who love Me, and those who seek me diligently will find Me. (Proverbs 8:17 NKJV)
- Draw near to God and He will draw near to you. (James 4:8)

Let's pray, "Heavenly Father, I seek You today. Today I put aside daily distractions, I put aside concerns, I put You first and know that when I search for You, I will find You! In Jesus' name, Amen."

Side note: We found the giraffe.

Put on every piece of God's armor...—
Ephesians 6:13 NLT

SUNSCREEN AND SWEATSHIRTS

BASEBALL MOMS HAVE THE SAME MOTTO AS Boy Scouts: Be Prepared!

Many tournaments ago, my fellow baseball moms and I sat in tank tops and shorts, drenched in a mixture of sweat and sunscreen, when everything changed. The clouds opened up and - out of nowhere - rain and hail (baseball sized - for real) pounded from the sky, forcing us to put on rain jackets and open up umbrellas. Next, a cold front hit. Out of nowhere. We piled on blankets and pulled sweatshirts out of our Mary Poppins bag of all-season clothes. In one day we'd gone from tank tops and baseball caps to sweaters and earmuffs. But we were prepared.

God, too, has specific instructions for what you should put on each day for whatever you may face. He wants you prepared. From head to toe, He has selected your spiritual outfit.

I picture Him standing outside your dressing room and saying Ephesians 6:13-17: "Put on every piece of

God's armor so you will be able to resist the enemy in the time of evil...

- **the belt of truth**
  God's promises are true. Seek truth and "put it on as your center."
- **and the body armor of God's righteousness**
  The body armor - often called the breastplate - protects the heart. Protect your heart with right living and right thoughts.
- **For shoes, put on the peace that comes from the Good News...**
  Stand in and on the peace you have in Him and in His word.
- **Hold up the shield of faith to stop the fiery arrows of the devil**
  Before you even see a "fiery dart" from the enemy, hold up that shield! Protect yourself with the faith you have in Him.
- **Put on salvation as your helmet**
  Always remember your salvation experience and the promises that came with it.
- **Take the sword of the Spirit, which is the word of God."**
  This is your weapon. The word of God is meant to destroy anything and everything that attempts to harm you. Take it. Use it. It always wins.

Let's pray, "Heavenly Father, let us put on Your spiritual armor daily. When we feel weak in an area, show us what piece may be missing so we can, once again, resist the enemy. In Jesus' name, Amen."

Seek the Kingdom of God above all else, and live righteously, and He will give you everything you need.— Matthew 6:33 NLT

BUT DADDY SAID...

I LOVED PLAYING IN THE SPRINKLER AS A child. You know, the sprinkler with an arched metal tube with tiny holes? The water would fan back and forth as we darted from side to side to stay wet. "We" was me and my cousin, Heather.

We'd play until one of us would want a turn squirting the other or splashing in the newly created mud hole under the tire swing. At that point, an argument might start over whose turn it was. All I had to do was say "Dad said..." or "Mom said..." and the argument ended. If Dad said it was time to come in, it was. If Mom said it was my turn to swing in the tire swing, it was. End of story.

The power of those words – their words – topped everything else. At that point, those words were all that mattered. I fully believe that uttering HIS words changes everything. And, while we talked about speaking – out loud – the word of God a few devotions ago, I really want to focus today on the power and authority of those words. HIS words. Literally, the words of your Heavenly Father.

Let's say to life, "Hey, Matthew 6:33 says if I seek God first that He will give me everything I need, even in what I'm going through." To say to the sleepless night, "Look, God said – that's right, GOD – that if I come to Him, He will give me rest. So there!"

The power of the word of God is just that – the WORD OF GOD. Do you realize you're speaking GOD's WORDS? Just like when the 8-year-old me proclaimed, "Daddy said...", the 40something me can say "God said..." and the same action, the same results, the same POWER is spoken to whatever I'm going through.

So what are you saying to and about whatever you're going through?

Let's pray, "Heavenly Father, I thank You for Your words. Your word says if I seek You first that You will give me everything I need. Today I seek You first. I put You first. You said will give me everything I need and I fully trust that. In Jesus' name, Amen."

With men this is impossible, but with God all things are possible.—Matthew 19:26 NKJV

MASSIVE BACKYARDS

I LIVE IN THE SAME TOWN WHERE I GREW UP. A few months back I decided to drive around and reminisce with Cole. We pulled in the alley behind the house where I spent those "sprinkler summers" I mentioned earlier. I pulled to a stop and stared in amazement.

"Cole, when I was 8 this backyard seemed huge. It felt like it took a lifetime to run from the back porch to the back fence. Now look at it. Now that I'm grown, it seems so small! How did I even fit a swing set back there?"

"Mom," my wise son chimed in, "when we're small, things seem so big."

It hit me, right then and there in that car, and I spoke to my son, "Son, how big is your God?"

"Mom, He's massive. He can do anything!"

"Yes, and when we have a problem, when life seems chaotic and we can't handle it, we can take it to our big God. Not only is it small to Him, but He can take care of it and of us and loves us with a big, huge love."

What's big to you? What are you hanging on to that you need to release to an even bigger, more powerful, loving God?

Let's pray, "Heavenly Father, thank You for taking care of me. I thank You that I can give an impossible, big, huge situation to You and You will take care of it. Today, I give my problems to You. In Jesus' name, Amen."

All Scripture is given by inspiration of God, and is profitable for doctrine, for reproof, for correction, for instruction in righteousness.—2 Timothy 3:16 NKJV

GIVING OUT Xs

DON'T TURN ME OVER TO DHS...

Cole bypassed the terrible twos and went straight toward the horrible, awful, rebellious threes. He'd run from me in stores, throw tantrums, and get red-faced all at the same time.

Still debating between spanking, a behavior chart, or time out, I exasperatedly exclaimed, "I'm going to give you an X!" after one of his episodes.

I didn't know what an X was, but apparently he did. That's all it took. I would threaten with "an X" and he would straighten up, quiet down, and obey my every word. Wow... this was going to be easy!

Until I watched a cartoon with him and realized that every time a cartoon character died, his eyes turned to big, black Xs.

Ugh. Y'all, my kid thought I was threatening to kill him.

SAY

Have you ever mistaken God's correction for something worse? Or maybe you've assumed that something bad that happened to you was from God.

Hold up! Just like I'm "for" Cole and want only the best for him, God, too, wants only the best for you. He's not up in heaven giving you Xs! The very word "discipline" comes from "disciple." Remember those guys? He adored them. They were His best friends!

So how, then, does God correct us? Well, it very well could be what you're reading right now. Chances are you've felt a little "ooh, that hit home" or "yikes, that hurt" after reading one of these devotions. His word says, "Scripture is for correction." So, where do you need correcting today?

Let's pray, "Heavenly Father, I thank You that Your word gently corrects and disciples me. Show me today where I'm wrong and where I need to change. In Jesus' name, Amen."

We walk by faith, not by sight.—
2 Corinthians 5:7 NKJV

CARNATIONS

AH, SCIENCE EXPERIMENTS. FOR SOME REASON, I love watching them. My son, too, found downloadable videos of lava-flowing, paper mâché mountains and of exploding, fizzy soda bottles.

One of my favorite experiments is from my teacher in preschool. You've probably done it too. A single, white carnation is placed in a clear glass of water. Blue food coloring is dropped into the water so the flower can soak up the blue dye. In a few days, the white carnation petals turn a beautiful, rich blue.

Now, if I placed a box around that glass of water so you couldn't see it and told you that my white carnation would turn blue, you wouldn't believe me, right? I mean, have you ever seen a blue flower?

In our spiritual walk, we must choose to walk by faith, not sight.

Sight says, "There's no way a flower can turn blue. It's not possible. I've never seen one."

Faith says, "I'm feeding this flower what it needs to turn blue. It will turn blue."

Sight says, "There's no way ___ can happen. It's not possible. I've never seen __ happen."

In our spiritual walk, faith says, "I'm feeding this situation with faith and the word of God. It will happen."

What are you telling your situation? What are you telling yourself? Are you walking by sight, by what you hear, by what the situation says? Or are you walking by faith and speaking the words of God over your situation?

Let's pray, "Heavenly Father, today I speak life to this situation (insert whatever it is here). I speak promises. I know You are for me and not against me and You want good for me. So even though I can't see evidence of You working, I know You are. I know this situation will work out for the good. In Jesus' name, Amen."

Oh, Lord... give us, Your servants, great boldness in preaching [proclaiming] Your word. —Acts 4:29 NLT

A CHALLENGE

AS WE NEAR THE END OF THIS BOOK, I WANT to challenge you. Assuming you've been praying out loud (the title of the book is "Say," not "Think"), you're used to hearing your voice be lifted to your Heavenly Father. If you're not used to it yet or, whoops, you haven't been praying out loud, feel free to re-read this until you feel a confidence to speak His promises over your life.

Hold this thought for a moment.

Joshua 10 tells the story of when Joshua himself prayed a prayer so big that it was humanly impossible. A miracle was required. The odds were stacked against him and his family and his country. In this story, Joshua didn't just pray out loud. Joshua 10:12 says "Joshua said to the Lord *in the presence of Israel...*"

He prayed this big, lofty, ginormous prayer where everyone could hear. He was their leader and they heard him pray to their God.

It's easy(ish) to pray "God, move this mountain" when it's just us and God. But what about a prayer so loud, so bold, that others know you're proclaiming and believing?

So, you guessed it... here's your challenge.

It's time to pray - to proclaim - so others can hear. Your children and family need to know your God and how to pray to Him. How will they know unless they hear you? How will they know unless you are that example? How will they know the power of the promises unless you proclaim them in their presence?

See, a few verses over, God answers Joshua's prayer and it was an answer that blessed the entire nation.

Who needs to be blessed from hearing you proclaim His promises?

Let's pray, "Heavenly Father, let us boldly come before You with praises, with prayers, and proclaiming Your promises. Give us wisdom and courage to allow others to hear that they, too, may be blessed. In Jesus' name, Amen."

**God causes everything to work together
for the good…**—Romans 8:28 NLT

BELIEVE IT OR NOT

ON SEVERAL TRIPS TO MISSOURI WE'VE
stopped at a Ripley's Believe It or Not museum. With
each replica of an anomaly or photo of a record-breaking
feat, you tilt your head and think, "hmmm, do I believe
it… or not?"

Over the past few days we've spoken blessings, proclaimed promises, and learned of His great love. We've
placed life storms against scripture and - each time - scripture won. But let me assure you of this: At some point in
the coming weeks (maybe in the coming minutes) you'll be
faced with the question, "Do I believe the promises, or not?"

Your answer to this question will determine the out-
come. Your actions based on your belief will hinder or help
you. Your decisions made at this very point will either open
the door to allow the already-given promises to flood your
spirit or will lock them out of sight.

But the medical report says…

But the judge says…

But my boss says…

But my ex says…

SAY

But God says... "I cause everything to work together for the good of those who love Me and are called according to the purpose I have for them." (Romans 8:28)

Now, what do *you* say?

"Heavenly Father, I am a masterpiece, wonderfully made to do good things. You have a purpose for me. Today I choose to capture fear-filled thoughts and align them with the Word of God which says if I stop worrying and, instead, pray about everything, tell God what I need, and thank Him for all He's done, I will experience God's peace. I give no room for Satan in my life. If I resist the devil, he is required to flee. I proclaim that the battle of financial burdens and of not-enough must go. I come today seeking God above all else. The word promises that when I do, my needs will be met. The storm of sickness and disease must go, because today I make You – Heavenly Father – my shelter and my refuge. I put my full trust in You and in knowing that when I do, no plague can come near my home. I have faith and I believe every prayer and every promise, knowing that You will cause everything to work for the good in my life. I love You and know that You will direct my steps when I trust and put You first. In Jesus' name, Amen."

I come to you in the name of the Lord!—
1 Samuel 17:45 NLT

RUNNING

HERE'S WHERE I COULD PREACH. I MEAN, THIS story is absolutely phenomenal and motivating and makes me want to get out and conquer whatever the enemy tries to throw at me. (Insert "Eye of the Tiger" here.) Okay, I just needed that image in your head. I digress...

So here's David. And David is minding his own business, which, at this point, includes tending sheep. His purpose is far greater than sheep, and he knows it. But what he doesn't know is that this field is a training ground for a big battle that is approaching.

David leaves his sheep and his field and goes to check on his brothers who, as David discovers, are being taunted and threatened by a massive warrior from the enemy Philistine army. This warrior - Goliath - freaked everyone out. Even the king.

But David heads straight to the scared king. "I'll go fight him!" David declares of the giant warrior. To which the king replied, "Don't be ridiculous."

Then something clicks with David. He realizes that all this time he spent taking care of stinky and stubborn sheep has paid off. The Bible said David *persisted* and told the king, "I have been taking care of my father's sheep and goats. When a lion or a bear comes to steal a lamb from the flock, I go after it with a club and rescue the lamb from its mouth. If the animal turns on me, I catch it by the jaw and club it to death. The Lord who rescued me from the claws of the lion and the bear will rescue me from this Philistine!"

After receiving the king's permission, the word says **"David quickly ran"** to meet and conquer the giant - the one that terrified all the experienced soldiers.

Everything God has brought you through may be preparing you for battle. This book may be showing you the authority and power within you to use God's promises to fight. And, friend, when you do head to battle, run. Run quickly toward whatever stands in the way of God's blessings!

Let's pray, "Heavenly Father, prepare me. Use me. Equip me. I thank You for where I've been and what You've brought me through. Make me ready for whatever stands in my way. Let me boldly and quickly run to Your promises and purpose. In Jesus' name, Amen."